AYO'S AWESOME ADVENTURES IN

NEW YORK CITY

THE BIG APPLE

www.worldbook.com

World Book, Inc.
180 North LaSalle Street
Suite 900
Chicago, Illinois 60601
USA

For information about other World Book publications, visit our website at www.worldbook.com or call 1-800-WORLDBK (967-5325).

For information about sales to schools and libraries, call 1-800-975-3250 (United States), or 1-800-837-5365 (Canada).

Library of Congress Cataloging-in-Publication Data for this volume has been applied for.

Ayo's Awesome Adventures
ISBN: 978-0-7166-3636-6 (set, hc.)

Ayo's Awesome Adventures in New York City: The Big Apple
ISBN 978-0-7166-4835-2

Also available as:
ISBN: 978-0-7166-3653-3 (e-book)

1st printing July 2018

Staff

Contents

Introduction

Are you ready for an adventure? I am! My name is Ayo. I'm an aardvark, an African mammal that eats ants and termites. I'm also a tour guide traveling the world. I hope you will come with me. In this book, we will visit New York City. It is the largest city in the United States.

The United States is on the continent of North America. I am from the continent of Africa. My name is an African word that means *joy.*

New York City has many nicknames. My favorite is the Big Apple. It sounds so sweet. The Big Apple is a very busy place, and there are so many things to do! We won't be able to see all of it. But I've visited this wonderful city many times. I think I can find plenty of fun things for us to do.

We'll be talking about many things that may be new to you. I'll try to explain any words you might not know as best I can. If a word cannot be explained very easily, or if I use it over and over again, I will put it in boldface. Boldface is type that **looks like this.** All boldface words will be defined in a glossary in the back of the book. Some words can be tough to say. If I use such a word, I'll be sure to sound it out slowly for you. Here's an example. You'll soon find out that New York City is divided into five boroughs. *Boroughs* is pronounced *BUR ohz.*

I hope someday you can travel with your family to New York City. You can ask to see the places we visit in this book! Then you can be the tour guide for your parents and brothers and sisters.

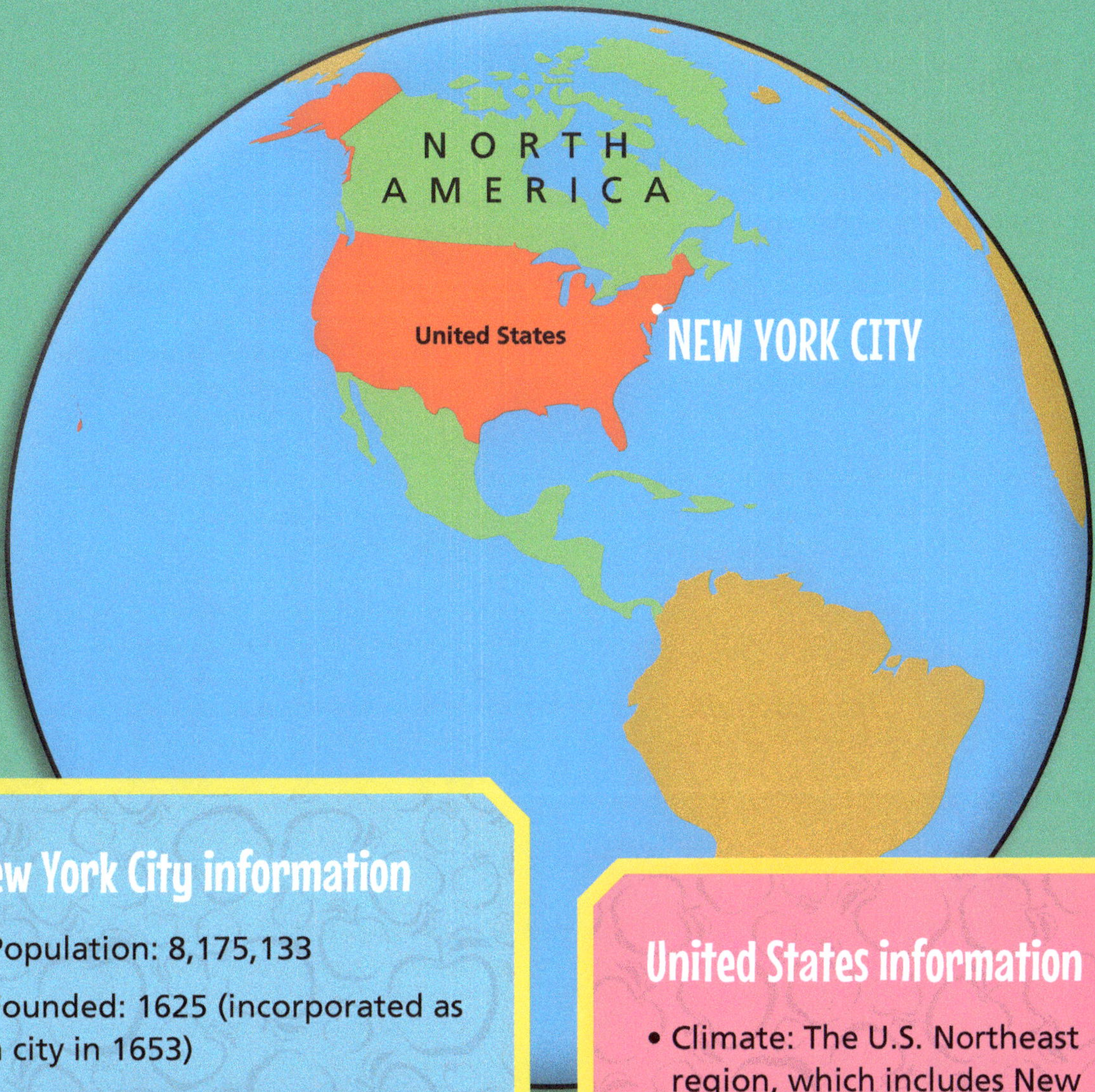

New York City information

- Population: 8,175,133

- Founded: 1625 (incorporated as a city in 1653)

- Economy: New York City is the most important place in the United States, if not the world, for many kinds of businesses. These include banking, *publishing* (making books and magazines), theater, and shipping, to name just a few.

- Restaurants: New York City has an amazing variety of restaurants—including Indian, Thai, French, and so on.

United States information

- Climate: The U.S. Northeast region, which includes New York City, has warm summers and cold, snowy winters.

- Money: U.S. dollar. One hundred cents equal one dollar.

- Flag: 50 white stars, for the 50 U.S. states, and 13 red and white stripes, for the original 13 American Colonies

flag of United States

Islands

I am excited to show you around New York City! Let's begin with an important fact about New York. It is mostly a city of islands. Each island has its own story.

The first people to reach the island of Manhattan were Native Americans. They found a lush forest full of wildlife. Settlers from Europe arrived in the early 1600's. They bought this little sliver of land from the Native Americans who lived and hunted there. How much do you think they paid? Legend tells us that the Europeans traded cloth and other trinkets worth about 24 dollars for the land. But the truth is probably a lot more complicated.

Soon, Europeans were settling on nearby Long Island, too. The Long Island settlements closest to Manhattan developed strong ties with Manhattan. By the way, Long Island is really long—120 miles (190 kilometers)!

Staten Island was mostly small farms until about 50 years ago. Then the Verrazano-Narrows Bridge was built in the 1960's. More people moved to the island. But even today, it isn't as crowded as Manhattan and the rest of New York City.

Ellis Island (pages 36–37) was where many **immigrants** officially entered the United States.

Liberty Island (pages 34–35) is home to the Statue of Liberty.

Boroughs and neighborhoods

New York City is a really big place. Let's take a look at how it is organized.

New York City is made up of five main sections. Each section is called a **borough** *(BUR oh)*. Remember when I said that most of New York City lies on islands? All but one of the boroughs are located on islands.

The boroughs are divided into neighborhoods—more than 100 altogether! **Immigrants** from the same country often settled, and still settle, in the same neighborhood. They brought with them their language and customs, giving many neighborhoods an international flavor.

We can get to almost every borough by using the **subway** system. Subways in New York even go under the East and Harlem rivers. To get to Staten Island, though, we have to ride the ferry.

The Five Boroughs

- Manhattan has the smallest land area of any of the boroughs.

- The Bronx is just across the Harlem River from Manhattan. It's the only borough not on an island.

- Queens and Brooklyn are both on Long Island. They share the western end of it.

- Staten Island has the smallest population of any borough.

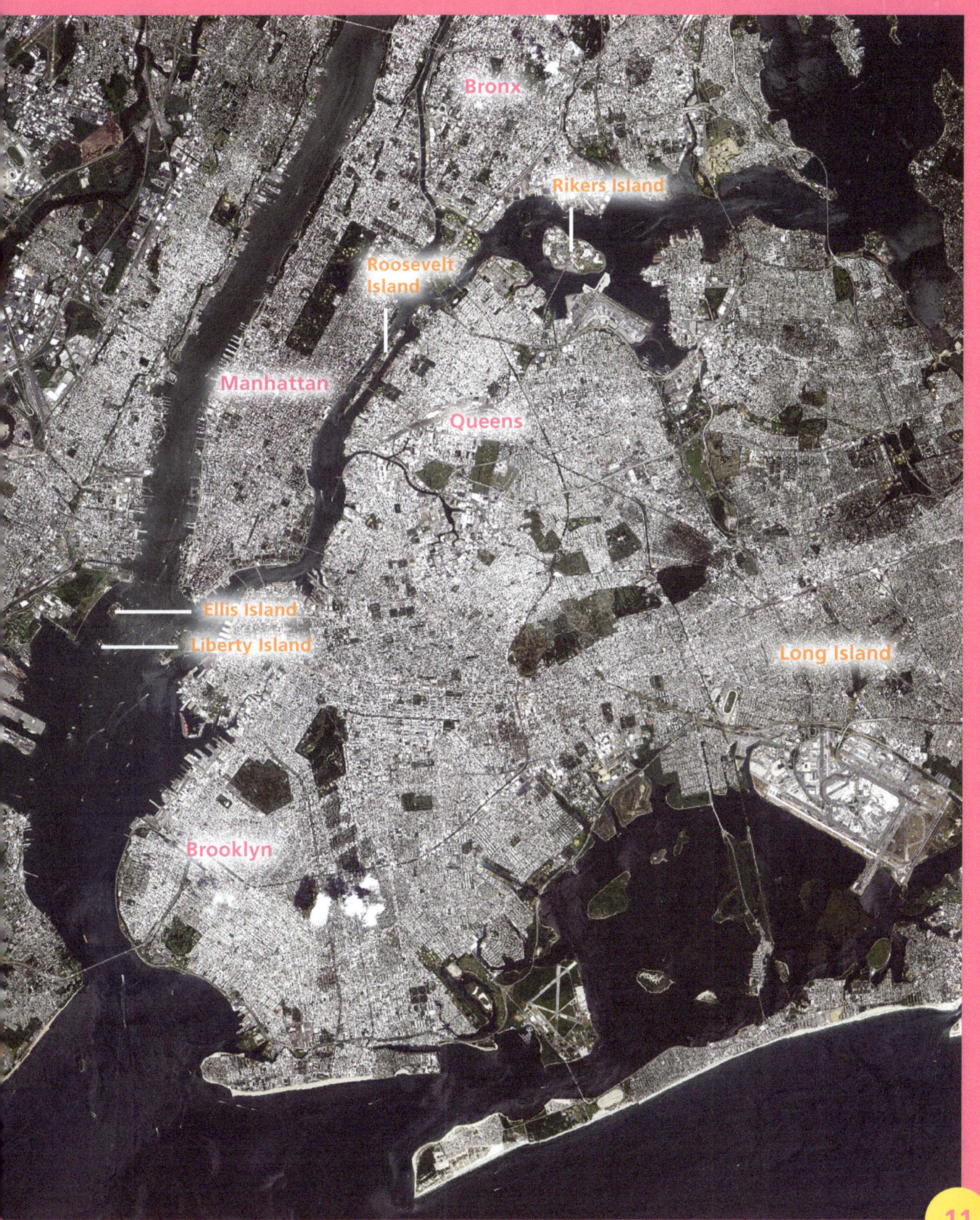

Bronx
Rikers Island
Roosevelt Island
Manhattan
Queens
Ellis Island
Liberty Island
Long Island
Brooklyn

Manhattan

There's a song about New York City that calls it the "city that never sleeps." In the **borough** of Manhattan, that may actually be true. There's always something to do, day or night. Even the **subway** runs 24 hours a day!

Manhattan has the tallest buildings in New York City. It also has some of the most important schools and colleges in the United States. Some of the richest—and some of the poorest—people in the United States live on Manhattan Island. And it has the most famous theater district in the world.

One of my favorite things to do here is to take a boat tour all the way around Manhattan Island. From the deck of a boat, the buildings look like mountains. Later, when we are in the streets of Manhattan, it will feel like we're walking in a canyon.

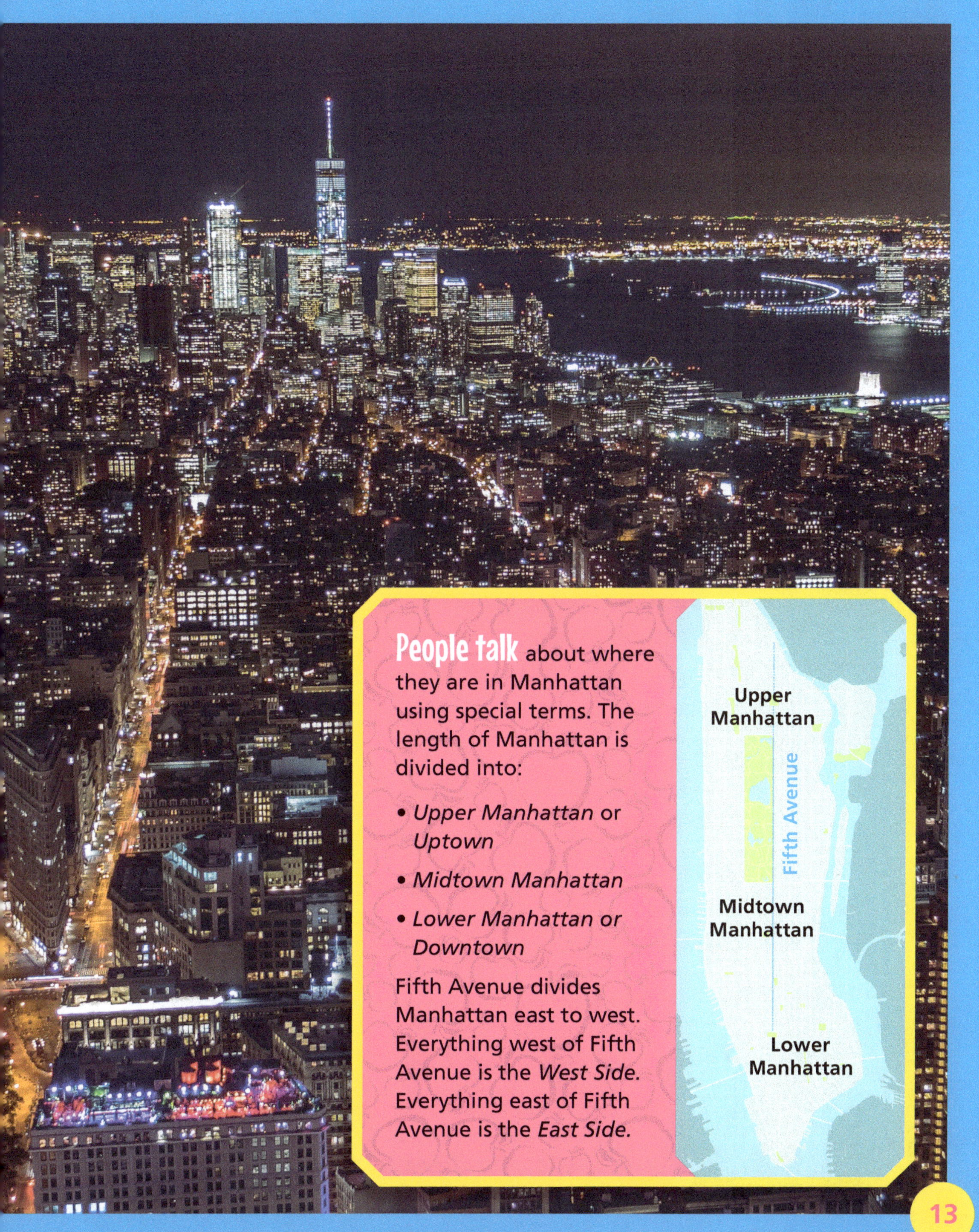

People talk about where they are in Manhattan using special terms. The length of Manhattan is divided into:

- *Upper Manhattan* or *Uptown*
- *Midtown Manhattan*
- *Lower Manhattan* or *Downtown*

Fifth Avenue divides Manhattan east to west. Everything west of Fifth Avenue is the *West Side*. Everything east of Fifth Avenue is the *East Side*.

Empire State Building

You know who has the best view of Manhattan? Birds. Aardvarks and kids are too close to the ground. But we can get a bird's-eye view from the Empire State Building. Let's head to Midtown.

The Empire State Building soars 1,250 feet (381 meters) over Midtown. It opened in 1931 and was the world's tallest building for 41 years. We'll take an elevator to the 86th floor (there are 102). An open-air observation deck wraps around the building. We can see in all directions! Let's use the high-powered binoculars to look at far-away things up close. Looking northeast we see the Chrysler Building. For awhile it was the tallest building in the world—until the Empire State Building was built.

looking
south
Chrysler
Building

Times Square

Do you remember what I said earlier? "The city that never sleeps"? Well, Times Square, here in Midtown, is a big part of the reason. It's so brightly lit at night, I might need sunglasses after the sun sets!

Times Square isn't really a square. It's formed where three streets come together: Broadway, Seventh Avenue, and 42nd Street. Broadway is also the name of the area around Times Square. There are a lot of theaters here. They attract big crowds in the evenings. The people come to watch musicals and other plays.

What can children and aardvarks do in Times Square?

- The Red Steps: 27 steps built over the TKTS booth (that's where you can purchase theater tickets). They lead to a platform from which we can look out over the sights of Times Square. Each step is lit from the inside, so the whole staircase glows a bright ruby red. It'll be much easier to see things from 16 feet 1 inch (almost 5 meters) high!
- Madame Tussauds New York: This museum displays famous people, such as music and sports stars, all sculpted from wax.
- New Victory Theater: It's New York City's only theater just for kids.

The Red Steps

Central Park

How about a stroll through Central Park? When we were looking out from the observation deck at the Empire State Building, it was hard to miss Central Park. It covers 50 city blocks—and it's green!

We'll enter the southern part of the park from Fifth Avenue. That puts us at the entrance to the Central Park Zoo, New York City's first zoo. Let's make sure to explore the Tisch Children's Zoo, tucked into the northeast corner of the bigger zoo.

Looks like we're not the only ones passing beneath the trees in the middle of the park. Skateboarders and bicyclers swoosh past us constantly. Did you know we can take a boat out on Central Park Lake? Or we could cross Bow Bridge and go hiking in the Ramble. The Ramble is a little forest— right in the middle of the big city!

There's less of a crowd in the northern end of the park. We can visit the turtle pond, then hike through a big garden.

At the zoo we can see more than 100 kinds of animals, from polar bears to poison dart frogs to penguins. Alas—no aardvarks!

American Museum of Natural History

New York is crammed with museums. We can't possibly see them all! Let's see one bursting with fun things to learn about life on Earth. The American Museum of Natural History has its own **subway** stop. You step out into the Upper West Side neighborhood, across the street from Central Park.

Inside, I like to go straight to the dinosaur wing. My favorites are *Tyrannosaurus rex* and *Triceratops*. You can choose your favorite from about 100 dinosaur skeletons.

If you visit December through May, head to the second floor and the Butterfly Conservatory. It's warm

inside the *vivarium,* an indoor enclosure for living plants and animals, and you get to hang out with hundreds of butterflies.

We can't leave without seeing the model of a blue whale. It's the same size as a real blue whale—about 94 feet (29 meters) long. That's as long as about 17 average aardvarks, if you could keep us still long enough to line up.

Back on the first floor, let's see what's playing at the Hayden Planetarium Space Theater. Most of the museum is about life on this planet. The space shows are about what's beyond Earth.

Greenwich Village

Aahh… isn't this nice? I… wait a minute. Where are we? Oh, right! Greenwich (*GREHN ihch*) Village. Every time I come to this neighborhood, I start to forget that I'm still in big, bustling New York City.

I love these narrow, tree-lined streets. There's nothing else quite like them in this city. Greenwich Village feels like a small town. Maybe that's because it used to be a country village, before the city overtook it.

I'd like to show you Washington Square Park, the heart of Greenwich Village. A tall marble monument called a *triumphal arch* honors George Washington, the first president of the United States. Hear all of that music? Lots of street musicians perform here. Some of them are really good. The neighborhood attracts all kinds of artists. Many painters, writers, and musicians got their starts here. Some of them, such as the singer Bob Dylan, are world famous.

Visitors sure do like to shop in New York—and Bleecker Street is a favorite place. Grown-ups like the guitar shops and boutiques. We might prefer the ice cream shops and bakeries.

Bedford Street in Greenwich Village is home to New York City's narrowest house. It's only 9 1/2 feet (2.9 meters) wide. That's about two aardvarks, measuring nose to tail.

Grand Central Terminal

As visitors, we zip around the islands on **subways** and **ferries.** Now let's see where *commuters,* people traveling to and from work, go to catch trains that take them to homes outside Manhattan.

Grand Central Terminal is huge! There are 44 separate platforms for trains to arrive and depart. That's more than any other train station in the world. And all of the train tracks are underground, on two levels.

We'll go in at the 42nd Street entrance so I can show you a nifty part of the building. Outside the entrance, near the roof, is a sculpture of three characters from Roman mythology.

Mercury (center): the god of travel, business, and wealth

Hercules (left): the son of Jupiter, who represents strength and hard work

Minerva (right): the goddess of wisdom

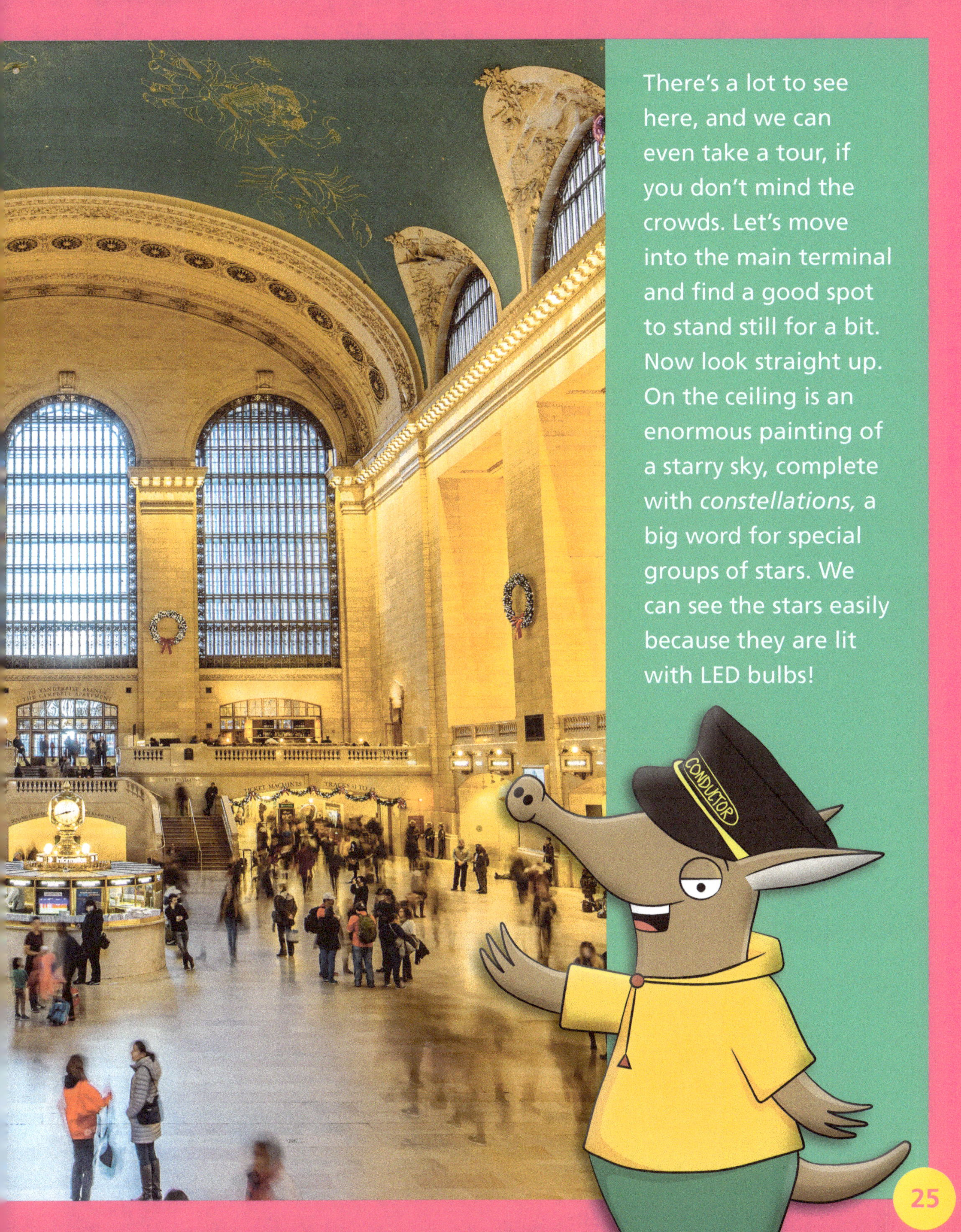

There's a lot to see here, and we can even take a tour, if you don't mind the crowds. Let's move into the main terminal and find a good spot to stand still for a bit. Now look straight up. On the ceiling is an enormous painting of a starry sky, complete with *constellations*, a big word for special groups of stars. We can see the stars easily because they are lit with LED bulbs!

Harlem

Let's take the **subway** to Uptown Manhattan, all the way to 125th Street. We'll be in Harlem.

We could spend days here in the center of African American culture. The neighborhood stretches almost from the Hudson River to the East River on the northern part of Manhattan Island.

Of all the museums, theaters, and restaurants, I'd like to show you the Apollo Theater. It's been around for more than 100 years! Many great entertainers have performed here. If it's Wednesday, we can go to "Amateur Night at the Apollo." And during the "Stars of Tomorrow" part of the show, you can go on stage and sing! If you aren't 15 yet, anyway. Don't worry about being booed—no booing is allowed.

Are you hungry yet? I am. Harlem is packed with different kinds of food. American hamburgers or crab cakes? Southern catfish? Cajun? French? Italian? You pick!

If you feel like swimming, playing soccer, or shooting hoops, we can head over to Riverbank State Park. There's even an ice rink in winter that turns into a roller rink in summer. Just remember, if anybody asks, I'm your tour guide, NOT your pet. (No pets allowed.)

Uptown and Downtown parks

Speaking of parks, there are two more I want to show you. One is in Downtown and the other is in Uptown.

First up, the High Line in Downtown Manhattan. This used to be part of an elevated train line. It ran through the city above street level. After the train line stopped running, weeds grew wild on the abandoned part of the tracks. Some people wanted to tear down the tracks. Then someone had an amazing idea: Why not turn it into an elevated park? The High Line is now one of the city's most popular walking paths. It's about a mile-and-a-half long and runs above 10th Avenue.

Fort Tryon Park is in Uptown—way up, near the northern tip of Manhattan Island. It used to be an army fort. Now we can wander through eight miles of **pedestrian** trails, explore two playgrounds, and check out the **borough's** largest dog run.

Fort Tryon Park even has its own museum. At the Met Cloisters, part of the Metropolitan Museum of Art, we can see parts of buildings as well as paintings from the *medieval* period in Europe. That means the things we'll see are from the 400's to the 1400's.

columns at the
Met Cloisters

The Financial District

We can take the **subway** to the southern tip of the island to visit one of the oldest parts of New York—the Financial District. The streets are narrow, but the buildings are big, and the business is even bigger. The world's money business is focused right here, on Wall Street!

Let's escape the traffic and head over to Stone Street. It is for **pedestrians** only. Some people I've talked to say it is Manhattan's oldest paved street. It's a little bumpy because it is paved with *cobblestones,* just like it was 350 years ago. Cobblestones are rounded bricks used for making streets. It's a short stretch filled with restaurants and shops at street level. The old brick buildings rise only a couple of stories above our heads.

Winding our way west, we will come to Bowling Green Park, the oldest park in the city. Do you recognize the famous bronze statue *Charging Bull?* It stands here as a symbol of confidence in the financial system.

The tangle of streets almost gets confusing, but I see daylight up ahead. This open green space, with the harbor in view, is called the Battery. This park sits at the southern tip of Manhattan Island. We can visit the Battery Urban Farm, catch the **ferry** to other islands, or just watch the bustle of New York Harbor.

The New York Stock Exchange *(shown here)* is the oldest exchange in the United States. In this marketplace, people buy and sell *shares,* or portions of the value of companies.

Freedom Tower

We couldn't come to New York City and the Financial District without visiting One World Trade Center. Many people call it Freedom Tower.

At one time, two skyscrapers stood near this place. The twin towers of the World Trade Center were the tallest buildings in New York. On Sept. 11, 2001, both buildings were destroyed by terrorist attacks. More than 3,000 people died.

Freedom Tower is now the tallest building in the United States. Lean back to glimpse the top, 1,776 feet (541 meters) in the sky.

The One World Observatory takes up three floors at the top of Freedom Tower. On the walls of the Sky Pod

National September 11 Memorial and Museum

elevator, we can watch how the city developed from wilderness to today's busyness. The show covers 500 years in 60 seconds.

We can look in all directions from the observatory. But I can show you an even more exciting view. It's a 14-foot (4.3-meter) glass disc called the Sky Portal. You can walk on it and look straight down—100 stories!

Across the street is the National September 11 Memorial and Museum. We'll learn more about what happened on Sept. 11, 2001.

The **height** of 1,776 feet honors the year the American Colonies declared independence.

Liberty Island

Can you guess what stands on Liberty Island? The Statue of Liberty! Let's take the **ferry** from the Battery to explore it. I hope you don't mind boat rides. The ferry is the only way to get there.

Do you have a nickname? The statue does: Lady Liberty. (Her real name is *Liberty Enlightening the World.*) She has been here since 1886. The French people gave her as a gift to the United States. The sculptor, Auguste Bartholdi, wanted his statue to face the ocean, so **immigrants** would see her welcoming them as they arrived.

The Statue of Liberty stands on a pedestal. Should we go up to Lady Liberty's crown? We'll have to climb 146 steps on a spiral stairway—after 231 steps from the lobby to the pedestal! There is no elevator to whisk us to the crown.

The statue looks like it's covered in green metal, doesn't it? That's actually copper. Over time, copper reacts with air to form a green coating.

Ellis Island

Since we're already at Liberty Island, let's take the **ferry** to Ellis Island. It's only a few minutes away. Ellis Island is an important part of New York City's history, and it explains a lot about the city.

The people of New York City have come from all over the world. In the 1800's and the early 1900's, many Europeans came to New York City. These **immigrants** saw the Statue of Liberty as they approached New York for the first time. But their first stop was Ellis Island. Between 1892 and 1924, all of these immigrants passed through Ellis Island.

Passing through an island—that sounds strange, doesn't it? You can find out what that was like for immigrant kids and their parents at the Ellis Island Immigration Museum. In the Baggage Room you can compare your backpack to the kinds of suitcases immigrant kids may have carried. In the Registry Room, also called the Great Hall, imagine standing in line for three to seven hours with hundreds of people. Lots of exhibits show how hard—maybe even kind of scary—it was to answer questions, get a medical check-up, and find your suitcase again.

Brooklyn

Just across the East River from Manhattan is Brooklyn. We can get there by crossing the Brooklyn Bridge. There's even a **pedestrian** walkway for kids and aardvarks.

Did you know that Brooklyn has the largest population of New York City's **boroughs?** About 2.5 million people live in Brooklyn. If Brooklyn were its own city, it would be the fourth largest city in the United States.

If you think that's big, wait until summer. More than 10 million people come to Brooklyn just to go to Coney Island! Let's head out there now. We can sit on the beach, go on amusement park rides, and find treats to eat and games to play on the boardwalk.

Does going to the beach get you thinking about life in the sea? I know a place nearby where we can see sand tiger sharks, sea otters, cownose rays, and colorful reef fish. What's your favorite sea creature? Maybe we can find it at the New York Aquarium.

People came to live in Brooklyn from many parts of the United States and the world. Sometimes they stuck together in their own neighborhoods. Let's see which groups are associated with which neighborhoods.

Bensonhurst: Italian Americans

Brighton Beach: Russians

Bedford Stuyvesant: African Americans

Queens, the Bronx, and Staten Island

Many visitors spend so much time in Manhattan that they barely even make it to Brooklyn. And there are three more **boroughs** to visit after that! I think we'll need to come back to New York. For now, I'll give you a quick tour of what to see in the Bronx, Queens, and Staten Island.

The Bronx

You know I like a good zoo, and each of these boroughs has one. But only the Bronx Zoo has a bug carousel. You can even ride a dung beetle! (But you can't ride an aardvark.) In cool weather, the carousel closes its sliding glass door to keep us warm.

Queens

At the New York Hall of Science, we can plunge our paws into activities and help out in science demonstrations.

Staten Island

Remember, we'll have to take a **ferry** to get to Staten Island. That's okay with me. I love riding the Staten Island Ferry!

At Historic Richmond Town, let's find out what life was like for kids and their families during the 1600's, 1700's, and 1800's. We'll tour such buildings as a tinsmith's shop and a basket maker's house and explore a working farm.

Sports

Our trip to New York City is coming to an end. But there's still time to do one more thing. Do you have a favorite sports team? Kids in New York have a lot of teams to choose from. You can pick one, too! You can get to the places where all these teams play by **subway,** bus, or train.

The Yankees play major league baseball at Yankee Stadium in the South Bronx. The Mets also play major league baseball, but at Citi Field in Queens. The New York Islanders play professional hockey at the Barclays Center in Brooklyn.

Three professional teams play at Madison Square Garden, in Midtown Manhattan. The New York Knicks play men's basketball. The New York Liberty are the city's professional women's basketball team. The New York Rangers play in the National Hockey League.

Do you like tennis? Then you probably know that the US Open Tennis Championship is one of the most important tournaments in the world. It's held every year around Labor Day at the Billie Jean King National Tennis Center. That's in Flushing, a neighborhood in Queens.

New Yorkers root for two professional football teams, the New York Jets and the New York Giants. But they don't play their home games in New York! We'd have to go to MetLife Stadium over in New Jersey.

New Yorkers also root for two professional soccer teams. The New York City Football Club plays at Yankee Stadium. The New York Red Bulls play at Red Bull Arena in New Jersey.

Times Square
Coney Island
Liberty Island
Central Park

Thanks for exploring New York City with me. I hope to see you soon!

Ayo

Glossary

borough (*BUR oh*) One of the five local units that make up New York City

ferry (*FEHR ee*) A boat used to carry people, vehicles, or cargo across narrow bodies of water

immigrant (*IHM uh gruhnt*) A person who comes into a different country to live

New Yorker (*noo YAWK kuhr*) A person who lives in New York City

pedestrian (*puh DEHS tree uhn*) A person who goes on foot; reserved for foot traffic

subway (*SUHB way*) An electric railway running beneath the streets of a city

Acknowledgments

Cover © Sean Pavone, Shutterstock
Ayo artwork by Matthew Carrington

4-9   © Shutterstock
10-11   JAXA/ESA
12-13   © StockMediaSeller/Shutterstock; © iStockphoto
14-17   © Shutterstock
18-19   © Melpomene/Shutterstock; © Castle City Creative/iStockphoto
20-21   © Andrea Izzotti, Shutterstock; © Timothy A. Clary, Getty Images
22-23   © Ryan DeBerardinis, Shutterstock; © Javen/Shutterstock; © dbimages/Alamy Images
24-27   © Shutterstock
28-29   © Ferrantraite/iStockphoto; © Manuel Hurtado, Shutterstock
30-31   © Kamira/Shutterstock; © Photo.ua/Shutterstock; © Sean Pavone, Shutterstock
32-33   © Bojan Bokic, Dreamstime; © Shutterstock
34-37   © Shutterstock
38-39   © Kamira/Shutterstock; © Louise Rivard, Dreamstime
40-41   © Danita Delimont/Alamy Images; © Citizen of the Planet/Alamy Images
42-43   © Leung Photography/Dreamstime

Index

For further reading

Books

[DK staff editors] *Family Guide: New York City.* Dorling Kindersley, 2016.

Fox, Kelsey, and Shiela, Leon H. *Kids' Travel Guide - New York City: The fun way to discover New York City - especially for kids.* FlyingKids Limited, 2016.

Websites

Parks in New York City
https://www.nycgovparks.org

Ellis Island and the Statue of Liberty
https://www.nps.gov/elis
https://www.nps.gov/stli

American Museum of Natural History
https://www.amnh.org